JUNGLES

Last Frontiers for Mankind
JUNGLES

Lawrence Williams

MARSHALL CAVENDISH
New York · London · Toronto · Sydney

Library of Congress Cataloging-in-Publication Data

Williams, Lawrence.
 Jungles / by Lawrence Williams
   p. cm. – (Last frontiers for mankind)
 Bibliography: p.
 Includes index.
 Summary: Describes the climate and plant and animal life of the jungles of the world and discusses the impact and effect of humanity in studying, invading, or destroying these jungles.
  ISBN 1-85435-171-0 (lib. bdg.)
  1. Jungle ecology – Juvenile literature. [1. Jungles. 2. Jungle ecology. 3. Ecology.] I. Title. II. Series:
Williams, Lawrence.
Last frontiers for mankind.
  QH541.5. J8G73 1990
  574.5'2642 – dc20   89-17322
                                                      CIP
                                                      AC

ACKNOWLEDGEMENTS

Maps and charts – Jillie Luff

Diagrams and illustrations – Outline Illustration, Derby – Andrew Calvert, Andrew Cook, Andrew Staples

Photographs – For permission to reproduce copyright material the authors and publishers gratefully acknowledge the following:

Cover photographs – main picture: West Itian, Asmat – inset picture – River Paku, Sarawak – Robert Harding Picture Library.

Page 4 – View over Amazon Jungle – Puttkamer, Zefa; page 5 – Deforested soil, Rondonia, New Amazon State – Hutchinson Library; page 8 – Gulley erosion of rainforest soil, St Lucia – Andrew Mounter, Planet Earth Pictures; page 12 – Tropical forest, Riverside, Brunei – Peter Scoones, Planet Earth Pictures; page 13 – Jungle, Queensland, Australia – Werner Frei, Planet Earth Pictures; page 15 (top) – Jungle, Oban, Nigeria – F. Sullivan, WWF–UK; (bottom) Harpy Eagle – L. C. Marigo, Bruce Coleman Limited; page 17 (left) – Korup National Rainforest Park, Cameroon, Africa – Phil Agland, Partridge Films Ltd; (right) Red and Green Macaw – Anna Culwick, TRees; Page 18 – Red Howler Monkey – Anna Culwick, TRees; page 20 – Dry leaf mimicry – Robert Harvey, TRees; page 21 – Robert Harvey, TRees, M. Rautkari, WWF–UK;

page 22 Amazon jungle – Tony Morrison, South American Pictures; page 23 – Giant Pangolin – Phil Agland, D. J. A. River Films; page 24 – A jelly fungus on fallen tree, Amazon – Tony Morrison, South American Pictures; page 25 – Dry hill rice planting, Malaysia – Richard Matthews, Planet Earth Pictures; page 26 – Whip Snake and Hyla Frog – Kevin Morgan, TRees; page 27 – Strangler – Tony Morrison, South American Pictures; page 28 – Mangrove swamp, Solomon Islands – Ben Burt; page 29 – Transitional forest, Peru – Robert Harvey, TRees; page 30 – Victoria Regia Lillies, Amazonia – Marion Morrison, South American Pictures; page 31 – Burning of Amazon jungle – J. V. Puttkamer, Hutchison Library; page 32 – Anaconda Snake, Riverside, Amazonia, Brazil, – Zefa, page 33 – Village in jungle, Southern Nigeria – Hutchinson Library; page 34 – Jungle clearance, Nicaragua – Mike Goldwater, Oxfam; page 35 – Jungle clearance by slash-and-burn, Peru – Anna Culwick, TRees; page 36 – Clearing Amazon Jungle – Hutchison Library; page 37 – Bougainville Copper Mine, Papua New Guinea – Planet Earth Pictures; page 38 – Buffer zone village, Cameroon – F. Sullivan, WWF–UK; page 39 (left) Medicinal plant garden, Tambopata Reserve, Peru – 'Tambopata Reserve Society'; (right) Extracting resin from Ójè tree, Tambopata Reserve, Peru – 'Tambopata Reserve Society'; page 41 (left) – Tarantula spider, Tambopata Reserve, Peru – Anna Culwick, TRees; (right) Toucan, Amazon Jungle, Brazil – Tony Morrison, South American Pictures; page 42 – Indians of Amazonian Jungle, Brazil – R. Halin, Zefa.

CONTENTS

INTRODUCTION

A view over part of the Amazon jungle. The river shown here is one of the many large tributaries of the River Amazon. The clouds developing over the jungle will give rain in the afternoon.

Jungles are evergreen tropical rainforests. Leaves fall from the trees and are replaced by new leaves every day of the year. There is no dry season and no winter in jungles.

Jungles grow in areas near the equator where there is rainfall all the year and temperatures are always high. The location of jungles is shown in the map on page 6.

Because jungles are **always** hot **and** wet, they are also very humid. There is always a lot of water vapor in the air. This steamy heat is just right for many species of plants and animals. Jungles cover only about four percent of the earth's surface, but nearly fifty percent of all animal and plant species live there.

The most striking fact about jungles is their **richness.** A hundred different kinds of tree may be found growing in an area the size of a football field. Living in and around these trees, there may be several thousand kinds of insects, birds and other animals. Fifty different kinds of insects may be found living in and on the bark of just one tree. This rich variety of life is much greater than in North American and European forests.

Jungles are a rich storehouse for the rest of the world. They contain the world's most valuable collection of hardwood trees. They also contain a great number of plants useful in medicine. Jungles offer scientists the chance to find out how different forms of life can live together.

But the jungles are in **crisis.** The opportunities that jungles offer to the peoples of the world are in danger of being wasted.

They are in danger from people's ignorance and greed. Jungles are being ripped out of the earth for their timber or to make way for farm cattle ranching, land and mining. Jungles are being cleared away so fast that about 250 acres (100 hectares) of trees are being lost every minute of the day and night.

The main danger is not from the few people who live in the jungles, but from outside. For example, Americans and Europeans are greedy for the good quality hardwoods in the jungles. They are greedy for some of the tropical fruits that can be grown on cleared land. They are also greedy for meat, especially for beef.

Jungles are now being cleared even faster than in the past. Greed is winning. The jungles are losing.

This book is about the crisis for jungles. It is about the possibility that they will be cleared from the earth in our lifetime. But this book is also about the beauty and richness of jungles and about efforts being made to **conserve** some of the jungles for the future.

Key words

conserve – To save what is good and valuable.

crisis – A turning point. Crisis may turn to danger or opportunity.

evergreen – Evergreen forests are green all year round. They are ever green. There is no fall season when all the trees are bare of leaves at the same time.

humid – Moist, damp. A lot of water vapor in the air. (See glossary page 44.)

location – Where a place is.

species – A group of plants or animals which can be classed together because they have similar features. A species can be distinguished from any other species. For example, there are several different species of parrots in the jungle.

tropical – Located between the tropics of Cancer and Capricorn. (See the map on page 6.)

Crop failure in Amazonia. Here, an area of jungle has been cleared, and the land is used to plant pineapples. But the crop has failed, and the plants have no fruit. One reason is that the deforested jungle soils are infertile. Another reason is that heavy tropical rainstorms have beaten down the plants and washed away much of the soil.

CHAPTER ONE

JUNGLES OF THE WORLD

LOCATION OF JUNGLES

Jungles lie in the tropical zone on and between the Tropic of Cancer and the Tropic of Capricorn. There are only a few areas which extend outside the tropics. They are in eastern Australia, northern Burma and the extreme southeast of Brazil.

The map shows this quite clearly. It also shows that jungles are located in three main blocks. These three hot, wet areas are:

South and Central America
Central Africa
Southeast Asia

In South and Central America, the biggest area is the huge extent of jungle in the basin of the River Amazon. It extends from the Andes Mountains in the west to the Atlantic Ocean in the east. It is by far the largest area of jungle in the world. Other areas of jungle are shown in eastern Brazil and Central America. They are separated from the main area. All these jungles of South and Central America together make up almost sixty percent of the world's jungles.

In Africa, the largest area of jungle lies on the west side in the basin of the Zaire River. It extends west along the coast as far as Guinea. There is also a patch of jungle on the east coast of Madagascar.

In Southeast Asia, the jungles stretch out of Asia to the southeast. They extend to many islands of the Pacific Ocean and into the northeast of Australia. Because these jungles are found on so many different land masses and islands, they show a great variety from place to place.

In several locations, the jungles, which are evergreen and have no dry season, pass gradually into nearby tropical forests, which are not evergreen and do have a dry season. Several of these areas are shown in the map.

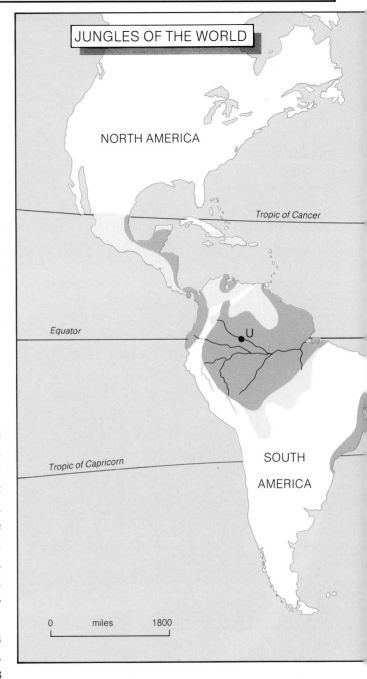

Many maps that have been drawn to show the location of jungles also show many disagreements. They show even more disagreements than between maps of deserts. There are several reasons for these disagreements.

1 Jungles are a special kind of tropical rainforest. But the boundary between jungle and another kind of tropical forest is not a clear line. For example, the jungle may change over many miles until it becomes a rainforest with dry season. (See diagram on page 31.) Mapmakers will dis-

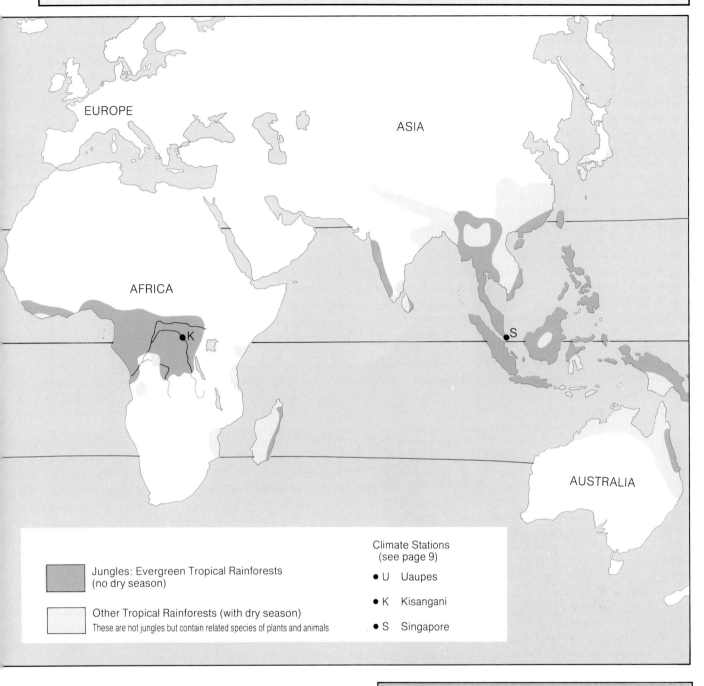

EUROPE

ASIA

AFRICA

• K

• S

AUSTRALIA

Jungles: Evergreen Tropical Rainforests
(no dry season)

Other Tropical Rainforests (with dry season)
These are not jungles but contain related species of plants and animals

Climate Stations
(see page 9)

● U   Uaupes

● K   Kisangani

● S   Singapore

agree where the boundary is. The map on this page shows two different kinds of forest, but some mapmakers want to put them all in the same group and call all of them jungles.

2 A second reason is that we still do not know very much about the richness of some jungle lands. For example, in South America, jungles enclose areas which are not really jungle at all, but have not yet been mapped separately. (See page 29.)

3 In some countries, jungles are being cut down so fast that a map is out of date by the time it appears in a book.

Look at the map on this page. Make a list of ways in which locations of jungles are alike. For example, most jungle areas extend to the sea.

Compare the map on this page with some atlas maps that give the names of countries. Make a list of countries that contain areas of jungle. You should have more than twenty-five names on your list.

CLIMATE OF JUNGLE LANDS

The climate of jungle lands is a tropical climate. It is a particular sort of tropical climate. It is hot and wet all year, and there is no dry season.

This tropical climate is clearly shown in the three graphs on page 9. (You can find out where these three places are by looking back at the map on pages 6 and 7.)

Temperatures

Temperatures are high all year. The three graphs show that, in all these places, average monthly temperatures never fall below 75°F (24°C), and do not rise above 82°F (28°C). This means that the annual range of temperature is only about 7°F (4°C). Temperatures can be described as **uniformly high.** There is no cold season as in North America and Europe.

The largest temperature differences are

St. Lucia, West Indies. This photograph shows how gully erosion can destroy a soil. Here, the jungle was cut down and the soil left unprotected from the heavy tropical rainstorms. Gullies like this can be eroded in only a few hours of heavy rain.

not between summer and winter, but between **day and night.** Differences larger than 77°F (25°C) have been recorded. This difference has led to the saying: "Night is the winter of the tropics." This is one way jungles are like deserts. But, as far as rainfall is concerned, jungles are nothing like deserts.

Rainfall

Once again, the three graphs show that the jungle lands are alike. Annual rainfall totals are high, and there is a large amount of rainfall in most months. Even at Kisangani, Zaire, where the average January rainfall total is only 2in. (5cm.), there is certainly not a dry season. The season from December to February is best described as the "least wet" season. Generally, most months in all three places see more than 4in. (10cm.) of rainfall.

This combination of high rainfall with high temperatures means that the climate is always humid and sticky.

Rainfall shows a clear **daily** pattern in most jungle lands. Clouds begin to form over the jungle in middle and late morning. (See the photograph on page 4.) By early afternoon, the clouds have built up rapidly, and violent rainstorms occur. In many places, these storms may give as much as 2in. (5cm.) of rain in one afternoon. The storms may end as suddenly as they began. The evening is cooler with clearer skies.

Sometimes, these storms, accompanied by thunder and lightning, can last for 24 hours. In these exceptional storms, some places have recorded as much as 20in. (50cm.) of rain in 24 hours.

These violent rainstorms do great damage to any areas of soils not protected by the dense vegetation of the jungle. Great gullies can be cut in a few hours. Whole fields can have the soil washed away in a sheet of water. The photograph on this page and the one on page 5 show different effects of rainwater erosion on unprotected soils. For a short time, rivers may be turned red by the soil washed into them.

At other times, most jungle areas have occasional short, dry spells. They may last for as much as two weeks. During this time,

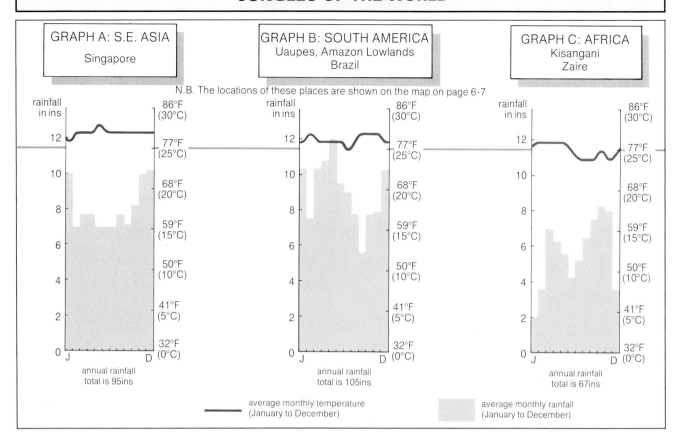

GRAPH A: S.E. ASIA
Singapore

GRAPH B: SOUTH AMERICA
Uaupes, Amazon Lowlands
Brazil

GRAPH C: AFRICA
Kisangani
Zaire

N.B. The locations of these places are shown on the map on page 6-7

annual rainfall
total is 95ins

annual rainfall
total is 105ins

annual rainfall
total is 67ins

─── average monthly temperature
(January to December)

▓ average monthly rainfall
(January to December)

jungle plants struggle to survive on water already in the soil and in their leaves and trunks. These dry periods seem to encourage some plants to burst into flowering and fruiting.

The lack of marked seasons, as they are known in North America and Europe, means that jungle plants do not shed all their leaves at one time. Most shed some leaves in all months and are producing new leaves most of the time. The effect of this is that the jungles are evergreen. (There are some deciduous trees which shed all their leaves at one time, but there are very few of them.)

As a result, the jungles experience not only uniform temperatures and rain in all seasons; they are also evergreen the whole year.

The three climate graphs tell a clear story about jungles. But they do not tell the whole story. The graphs are based on recordings of rainfall and temperature made in clearings where the instruments could be set up. What happens deep inside the jungles is rather different. These local climates, or micro-climates as they are called, are discussed on the next page.

Key words

average – The result of adding up some figures and dividing the answer by the number of figures. For example, if at Kisangani (Graph C), the thermometer is read six times a day in June, this means 180 readings in a month. Added together and divided by 180, the figures give 77°F (25°C) as the **average** monthly temperature for June. (Average temperatures are worked out over at least 35 years.)

deciduous – Shedding leaves annually in one season.

erosion – The breakdown and removal of rocks or soil. (See the photograph on pages 5 and 8.)

range – Difference between two values. For example, the average annual **range** of temperature in Singapore (Graph A) is the difference between May 82°F (28°C) and January 79°F (26°C). The average annual range is 3°F (2°C).

shed – To drop, cast off.

CLIMATES INSIDE THE JUNGLES

The inside of a jungle is a dark and mysterious place. It is cut off from the outer world by a complete cover of treetops called the canopy. A few trees may grow up through and above the canopy. They are called emergent trees. The trees of the canopy can be seen in the photograph on page 15.

The jungle is also enclosed at the edges. A dense growth of plants makes the jungle difficult to enter. This growth at the jungle edge is shown in the photograph on page 12. Anyone wanting to enter the jungle must cut their way in. Once they are inside the jungle it is much easier to travel. Between the trunks of the big trees, only shade-loving plants will grow. The jungle floor may be quite easy to cross. Because of the way the canopy and the jungle edges form a continuous unbroken cover, jungles are known as closed forests.

Inside this closed forest, the climate of the jungle lands is changed. This is shown in the diagram on the opposite page. Each layer of the jungle has its own microclimate. Each microclimate makes a special environment. In each environment, different species of plants, animals and birds are found.

Studying these different environments is not easy. Towers and rope walkways must be built high in the jungle. This has been done in only a few places. So we still know very little about these different environments.

The canopy acts as a kind of umbrella. This layer has the maximum rainfall. All the layers below it receive very much less. Only small amounts of rain fall through all the layers to the jungle floor.

Much the same thing happens with sunlight. The canopy trees receive almost 100 percent of available sunlight. But parts of the jungle floor receive only about 2 percent. Only shade-loving plants can survive on the floor.

In a similar way, it is the upper layers of the jungle that experience the biggest range of temperature. The lower layers are protected from the greatest extremes of high day-time temperatures and lower night-time temperatures. The same effect also applies to winds. There may be very little flow of air at ground level even when the canopy is enjoying a strong breeze.

EMERGENT TREE LAYER

These are very large trees emerging through the canopy. The climate here is similar to the tropical climate described on pages 8 and 9.

150ft (45m)

THE CANOPY

This is an unbroken cover of treetops. It acts like an umbrella for the rest of the jungle.
At the top the microclimate is like that of the emergent layer. There is nearly 100 percent of available sunlight. The largest daily ranges of temperature are here, sometimes as much as 80°F (25°C). Rainfall is heavy. The effects of the winds are strongest here. Only humidity is relatively low.
Passing through the canopy there is a dramatic change.

Towards the bottom of the canopy very little sunlight is available, often only about 5 percent. Also daily ranges of temperature are much less here between 40°F (5°C) and 50°F (10°C).
Very little rainfall passes right through the canopy to this level, probably only about 5 percent.
Effects of the winds are very much reduced to not much more than a gentle flow of air when there is a strong breeze above the jungle. Humidity shows a marked increase at this level.

82ft (25m)

UNDERSTORY
This layer is known as the understory. It can be divided into:
LOWER TREE and SHRUB AND FIELD

LOWER TREE
The microclimate here is humid and shadowy. Little sunlight and rain reach this level. The small trees are specially adapted to these conditions.

SHRUB AND FIELD
The microclimate here is even more marked by high humidity, lack of light, rain or airflow. Plants are specially adapted to the conditions. They are found where very small amounts of sunlight reach this level. Much of the jungle floor is open and easily crossed.

0ft (0m)

FOREST FLOOR
The microclimate is of very high humidity and still air. Only about 2 percent of sunlight and rainfall ever reach the floor.

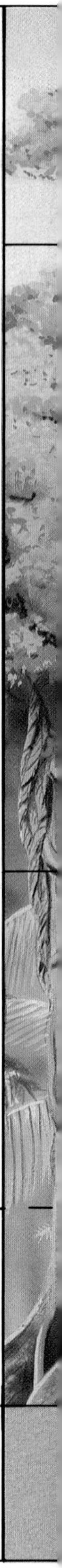

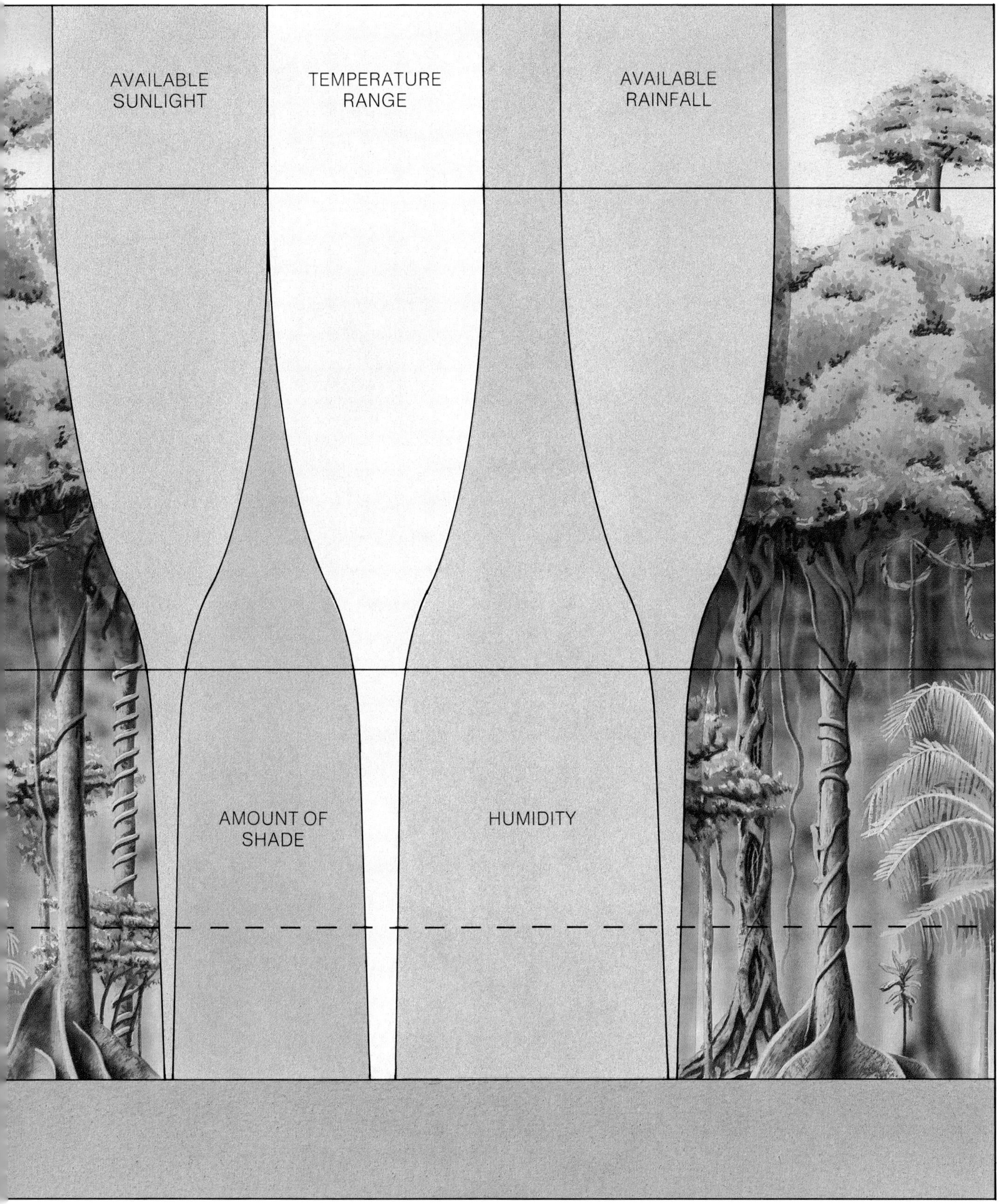

AVAILABLE SUNLIGHT	TEMPERATURE RANGE	AVAILABLE RAINFALL

AMOUNT OF SHADE

HUMIDITY

There is one important element of jungle climate that shows a marked increase **toward** the ground, and that is humidity. The amount of water vapor in the air at ground level may be very much more than at canopy level. The air is most humid in the still and sheltered lower layers.

Thinking about the jungle as a number of layers is one way of understanding the richness and variety of jungle life.

CHAPTER TWO

LIFE INSIDE THE JUNGLES

REACHING FOR THE LIGHT

All jungle plants depend on light for their life. The light received is used as energy in plant growth. Trees, shrubs and plants of every kind struggle to reach up to the light.

In this struggle for light, jungle plants can be divided into three groups.

1 The winners

This group includes all the trees of the canopy and the emergent trees that grow even higher. The large photograph on the cover gives a clear picture of this group, seen from the air. Because the canopy is usually complete, all plants below it are in shade. (See the diagram on page 10.)

2 The losers

This group includes all the plants that are outgrown and left behind by their stronger neighbors. The losers wither away and die. They collapse onto the jungle floor. There, they are soon broken down into humus by the insect and animal life of the floor. Their remains become food for the winners.

3 The adapters

This group includes all the plants that have developed ways of surviving in the deep shade below the canopy. They can be put into three groups.

a) Trees and shrubs with specially adapted leaves and trunks. They need very little direct sunlight.

b) Parasites are plants that life off other, more successful growing plants. They draw food out of the plants that they grow on. They are rooted on them.

c) Epiphytes are plants that use other, taller

The edge of the jungle at the riverside, Brunei. This photograph shows the effect of light and water on jungle plants. A complete wall of trees and shrubs cuts off the jungle from the outer world. The dark interior of the jungle is completely hidden. Note the many lianas hanging from the trees.

Jungle in northern Queensland, Australia. The struggle for light and space is shown by this mass of twisted branches and lianas.

and stronger plants to support them. They use them as props. (See the photograph on page 27.) Epiphytes draw their raw material for food directly from the air, raindrops and water vapor in the air.

One result of this struggle for light is that sometimes the jungle takes on the layered structure shown in the diagram on page 11. But, in many places, this simple structure is altered by other changes. For example, the death and collapse of an old canopy tree may make a large clearing open to the sky. The struggle for light begins again, and the layered appearance may be lost. (See the photograph on this page.) This kind of change and others like it are discussed on pages 20 and 24.

Reaching for light puts the plant life of the jungle in a state of crisis. The struggle is a life-and-death battle that never stops. But it is not only plant life that is involved. A rich variety of animal, bird and insect life depends on the plants of the jungle.

Relations between all these forms of life are very complicated. In many jungle areas, scientists have only begun to study these relationships in the last few years. The tragedy is that some jungles are being destroyed so quickly they will be lost before we learn to understand them.

Key words

energy – What is needed for doing work. In this case, the work is changing light energy to food energy for plant and animal growth.

epiphyte – A plant that uses another as a prop. It gets its raw material for food directly from air and rain. It does not weaken the other plant by feeding on it.

humus – Plant and animal remains that have been broken down and contain materials (nutrients) for use as food for living plants.

parasite – A plant or animal that grows and feeds on another. The other plant or animal, the one fed on, is known as the host. Hosts may be weakened by their parasites.

tragedy – A very sad event.

THE EMERGENT TREES

The emergent trees are the tallest trees in the jungle. They stand above the canopy layer. In the struggle for light, they have been the most successful trees. The photograph on page 15 shows how the emergent tree on the right stands above the level of the canopy trees. There is another example in the middle distance.

Emergent trees have almost no side branches below the canopy. Their branches are at the top, where the main branches divide into many small, thin side branches. As a result, most emergent trees are very top-heavy. They are supported by buttresses at the base of the trunk. (See the photographs on pages 17 and 22.) They are also held up by the canopy trees around them. When jungle is cleared around emergent trees, they sometimes fall over in the first strong wind.

Emergent trees are very large, but not nearly as tall as trees in other parts of the world. For example, the African mahogany tree (*Entandrophragma cylindricum*) rarely reaches 200ft. (60m.) in height. But the California redwood tree (*Sequoia sempervirens*) often grows up to 350ft. (105m.) It is also untrue that jungle emergent trees are the oldest in the world. Many other forest lands have trees five or six times as old as the oldest jungle trees. What **is** special about the emergent trees of the jungle is that they grow very, very fast in the hot wet climate.

The tops of the emergent trees grow in the most open environment of the jungle. (This was discussed in Chapter 1.) The treetops receive the most sunlight, the most rain and the most wind of any part of the jungle. The trees are adapted to these conditions in the ways they grow. For example, some trees have leaves with a waxy coating, which cuts down water loss by evaporation. Other trees have winged seeds which can be carried great distances above the canopy.

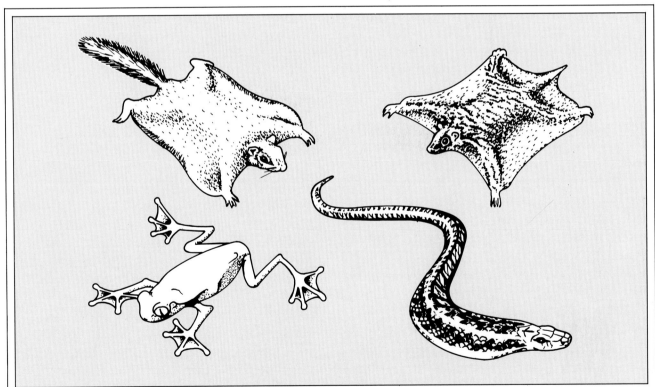

In the jungles of Southeast Asia and northern Australia live several different kinds of **gliding** animals. They live high up in the canopy and are often hunted by eagles.
The flying squirrel (*Acrobates pulchellus*) and the Colugo (*Cynocephalus variegatus*) glide on flaps of skin. Colugos have been recorded gliding as far as 444ft. (135m.) while losing height of only 40ft. (12m.). Other animals that can glide include frogs with webbed feet. There is also a snake that can flatten its body like a wing and glide between branches.

A view above the canopy of the jungle at Oban, Nigeria, West Africa. Emergent trees can be seen growing above the general level of the canopy.

Living in the tallest trees are the great hunters of the jungle: the eagles. The biggest and most ferocious eagle is the harpy eagle of Amazonia (*Harpia harpyja*). But all the main jungle areas have eagles living there. For example, the crowned eagle (*Stephanoaetus coronatus*) is found in Africa. And in the Philippines in southeast Asia, the monkey-eating eagle (*Pithecophaga jefferyi*) is found. All these eagles kill their prey with their massive claws and sharp beaks.

They feed off any animals that show themselves in the top of the canopy. Their favorite food is small monkeys, but they will eat other animals living in the treetops, including flying squirrels and colugos. If their prey tries to escape by dropping down to lower branches, the eagles may crash-dive at full speed through the top branches to catch their prey. Most eagle prey are animals attracted to the treetops by the flowers and fruits growing there. But if few of these animals can be caught, eagles will swoop down into jungle clearings and catch small ground-living animals instead. The Philippine monkey-eating eagle has a bad reputation among jungle people, because it will sometimes fly down and carry off their small pigs, poultry and even dogs.

Harpy Eagle *(Harpia harpyja)* **Amazonia**. This is the most powerful and largest of all the world's jungle eagles. But like even the weakest animal, it is threatened with extinction as more and more jungle is destroyed.

Key words

Note that when the proper zoological name of an animal is given, it is written in italics. This is the name by which the animal will be known in zoos and in zoological books and pictures.
For example, the harpy eagle is the common name for the Amazonian eagle which has the zoological name *Harpia harpyja*.

THE CANOPY

The tops of the canopy trees have an environment quite unlike any other in the jungle. It is really a series of environments from the bright, open, upper level to the dark, shaded underside. Another special feature is that many of the trees have their branches intertwined in their neighbors' boughs. They are also tied together by many kinds of creepers. The canopy is unbroken.

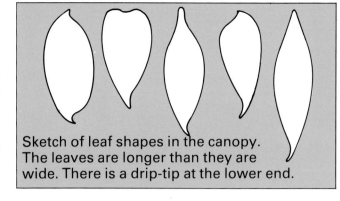

Sketch of leaf shapes in the canopy. The leaves are longer than they are wide. There is a drip-tip at the lower end.

One important result is that many of the animals that live in the canopy can travel a long way and find all the food they need without ever climbing down to the ground. The canopy is the safest place for many creatures in the jungle.

The canopy trees themselves fit into this environment in several ways. Here are some examples. Each example is known as an **adaptation.**

1 There is a great variety of species of canopy trees, but many of them have similar shaped leaves with smooth, shiny sides. The leaves are longer than they are wide with a pointed tip. The pointed tip is sometimes called the drip-tip. (See the drawing on this page.) This shape and smoothness encourages the rapid run-off of rainwater from the leaves. This is important in such a wet climate. It is interesting to note that drip-tips are longer in the wettest jungles.

But there may be a second reason for this adaptation. Some scientists now believe that, in the more humid parts of the canopy, leaves may be affected by mosses that grow on damp surfaces. Many canopy trees keep the same leaves for a year or more. So, if leaves did not get rid of water quickly, they might be damaged by growing mosses. Some trees would die. (It is interesting to note that very few emergent trees show this adaptation. It is also true that emergent trees have very different leaf shapes on the different species of tree.)

2 A second interesting adaptation is that although nearly all the canopy trees are evergreen, they are not producing new leaves all the time. A tree will produce a lot of new shoots and leaves at one time, and then wait several months before producing any more. This adaptation may be a way of preventing all the juicy new leaves from being eaten. If a few new leaves were being produced all the time, the hungry leaf-eating animals and insects would eat them all as they grew. If a lot of new leaves are produced at the same time, many of them will survive because the leaf-eaters cannot manage to eat such a huge feast. By the time the leaves are older and tougher, fewer creatures want to eat them.

3 A similar adaptation is shown by some trees of the same species, all of which flower and then fruit at the same times as each other. This increases the chances that some of the seeds will survive to produce a new generation of trees. This adaptation happens in a climate that does not have seasons like the climates of North America and Europe.

Adaptations of these kinds help trees to survive and spread. But the growth of new trees is also affected by the creatures that live in the trees. The trees and all the creatures living in them form a **community.** They depend on each other. For example, the trees provide homes and food for the animals and birds. The animals and birds help to spread the seeds from the trees.

Many birds live in the canopy. Parrots and hornbills are especially well known. Bird droppings contain seeds from the fruits and nuts they have eaten. The droppings themselves may act as a cover on the seed that discourages some ground insects from eating them. In other cases, the droppings might even act as fertilizer for the seeds.

Because this happens so often, some scientists believe that the spread of the jungle in the past might have been helped by parrots and other birds flying into new areas. But because plants and birds are **interdependent** in the community, the opposite might be true as well. The spread of jungle might encourage the spread of parrots into new areas.

Parrots, toucans and hornbills are just three examples of birds that live in the canopy and the emergent trees. They have a number of related features in common.

1 They have very colorful plumage. Their plumage varies very much from one species to another. It appears to be designed to attract a mate rather than to be any kind of camouflage. (See the photograph on this page.) Most of these birds are large and strong. Some of them are also able to fly fast.

2 Because the canopy vegetation is so dense, many of these birds have short, broad wings so they can fly between the branches. Also, many have feet specially suited to grasping the branches. They have two forward-facing and two rear-facing toes. As a result, they are good branch runners and climbers and do not fly everywhere.

3 These birds also have beaks adapted to help them with their feeding. Their beaks are adapted in different ways and look very different. This probably reflects their various diets. Some beaks seem designed to crack nuts, others to eat leaves and insects. (See the drawing on this page and the photograph on page 15).

Animals also help with the spread of seeds. One group, the sloths of the Central and South American jungles, are especially im-

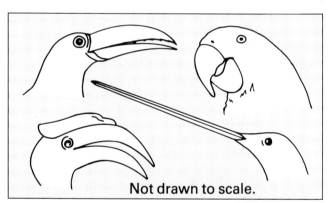

Not drawn to scale.

Buttresses of a giant tree in the Korup National Rainforest Park, Cameroon, Africa. This giant tree reaching up to the canopy and beyond is supported at the base by the buttresses. Note how climbers and lianas use the tree trunk for their support. In this area, the canopy is unusually open, and some sunflecks reach the smaller plants of the understory.

This is a red and green macaw. (*Ara chloroptera*).

portant. Their droppings are hard and protect the seeds inside.

There are several types of sloth. They live in the canopy, where they hang from the branches by all four limbs. They move very slowly and gracefully while hanging upside down. (Their slowness explains their name.) They are almost helpless on the ground because they have difficulty standing and walking. They would easily be victims of the jungle floor predators, especially the cats and snakes.

Six types of sloth behave like birds in allowing their droppings to fall from the trees to the ground. But the three-toed sloth climbs all the way to the ground, digs a hole with its tail, relieves itself in the hole, and then covers it with earth rather like a cat does. No one knows why this particular sloth risks its life in this way. But this behavior is a very good way to prepare for a new generation of jungle plants. (What a pity there is not the slightest evidence that the three-toed sloth knows it is doing this!)

Very different from the sloths are the monkeys. They can move fast and are good examples of the fact that most animals living in the canopy are **branch runners.**

Monkeys and some apes also show adaptations to living in the canopy. The most interesting fact about these adaptations is that some of them are different for different jungle areas. Here are some examples.

1 **Southeast Asia**
Gibbons are apes found only in the jungles of Southeast Asia. One of the ways they differ from other apes is that they have very long arms, about twice as long as their bodies. Their hands are also specially shaped and very strong. They are able to swing from branch to branch in the canopy. They use their arms more than their feet when traveling.

2 **Africa**
Most African monkeys are smaller than the gibbons of Southeast Asia. African monkeys are very graceful in shape and movements. Their arms are not as long as the arms of gibbons, and they use their feet much more in branch running. Unlike gibbons and other apes, most species of monkey have long tails which they use almost like a rudder when they leap through the air. *Colobus polykomos*, the black and white colobus monkey, has a beautiful plumed tail that it can use this way.

Howler Monkey (*Alouatta Seniculus*). The usefulness of the prehensile tail is very clear.

3 South America

Some of the monkeys of the South American jungles show an important adaptation not found in other jungles. They are prehensile-tailed. This means they use their tails as a fifth limb. (See the photograph on page 18.) They can hang onto branches as easily with their tails as with their hands and feet. This makes movement and the collection of fruit and nuts very much easier.

The largest South American monkey is the howler monkey. (See the photograph on page 18.) It gets its name from a second adaptation. Because of the shape of its mouth and larynx, its voice is so loud it can be heard miles away. Howlers live in troops of about twenty monkeys, and each troop has its own territory. Troops shout at each other as a way of marking out their own space.

These adaptations are concerned with **survival.** They help monkeys and apes avoid their enemies, such as the eagles. They help with the collection of food and the defense of their territories. But the adaptations cause us to ask another interesting question. Why are the adaptations different in the three jungle areas? (These three areas are shown in the map on page 7.)

Once again, we have no clear answer. One possible explanation is connected with continental drift. The great land masses of the world were once all connected. Then, millions of years ago, they began to drift apart very slowly. When they were connected, it is possible that all the jungle monkeys were alike. After the continents drifted too far apart for animals to move from one to another, the monkeys began to evolve differently in the different jungles. Why they should do this is not clear. It may be connected with slight differences in the now separated jungle lands.

However, this does not seem to be a complete answer. Some biologists have pointed out that the adaptation of the tail as a fifth limb by monkeys in South America is so useful it is surprising it has not happened elsewhere. There is no reason why it should not be just as useful in African and Southeast Asian jungles. So far, no one has discovered any reason that might have prevented it from happening there.

It is not possible in a book this size to write about all the creatures that live in and around the jungle canopy. This is one reason why a reading list is given on page 43.

The trees, animals and birds which have been described here form a major part of the canopy environment. They are interdependent and form a community of living things. One of the features that enables them to survive together is their adaptations.

Key words

adaptation – An alteration that helps a plant or creature survive in its environment. Adaptations may be concerned with movement, camouflage, attack or defense, territory, food supply, shelter, producing a new generation.

community – The plants and creatures that make up the living part of an area. They live together.

continental drift – The theory of continental drift is that continents were originally joined together. For example, the east coast of South America fitted against the west coast of Africa. Over many millions of years, the continents very slowly drifted apart to their present positions. In the last fifty years, much evidence has been found to support this theory. There is also clear evidence that continental drift is continuing now.

evolve – To develop and change from an earlier form.

generation – Born at about the same time.

Note the use of words and phrases such as:
"Some scientists believe . . ."
"It may be . . ."
"Might be . . ."
Why are they used?

UNDER THE CANOPY: THE UNDERSTORY

The understory has two layers:
1   The lower tree layer (above).
2   The shrub and field layer (below).
These layers are shown in the diagram on page 10. The diagram makes it clear that the tree layer is called "lower" because it is lower than the canopy.

All of the understory is a place of shade, high humidity and only the slightest movement of air. Little rainfall and little sunlight reach the understory.

The lower tree layer is made up of trees which reach a maximum height of only 33ft. (10m.) There is usually a gap between the tops of these trees and the lowest branches of the canopy trees. Also the lower tree layer is not continuous like the canopy, but has many gaps in it. (See the photograph on page 22.) However, these lower trees are often tied to each other, and to the trunks of the canopy and emergent trees, by many kinds of climbing plants and lianas. (See the photograph on page 13.)

Most of the tallest trees of the understory are fully grown by the time they are about 33ft. (10m.) tall. They are adapted to a life spent entirely in shade. Their leaves make use of what little light there is. One of the

most important sources of light is sunflecks. These are the occasional flecks of sunlight that actually come down through the canopy. The photographs on pages 17 and 22 illustrate this effect. The understory leaves are adapted to process this source of light energy.

Young trees which might grow to become canopy or emergent trees are rare. They are found mainly where there is a break in the canopy caused by an old tree falling down.

The shrub and field layer is even more shaded than the lower tree layer. So few plants can live here that the jungle floor is easy to cross. It is only where there is plenty of light that the understory forms a barrier. (It is helpful to compare the photograph on page 12 with the one on page 22.)

Life in the understory shows two features similar to features in the other layers of the jungle:
1 Although the idea of jungle being in layers is helpful to our understanding, in reality it is not like that. Many forms of life live in more than one layer at a time. Here are some examples involving the understory.
   a) Many climbing plants link the field layer to all the others, even to the top of the emergent trees. Some epiphytes and parasites do this. (See the photographs on pages 12 and 13.)
   b) The many species of bat which live in the understory trees are just as much at home in the underside of the canopy trees.
   c) The larger animals found in the lower tree layer frequently move down to the floor in search of prey. Examples include the clouded leopard *Neofelis nebulosa* (Southeast Asia), the jaguar *Panthera onca* (South America) and the bushmaster snake *Lachesis muta* (South America). However, they avoid sleeping on the jungle floor and return to the branches of the understory or even the canopy at night.
2 Almost every life form shows special adaptations to the conditions. But in the understory, adaptations are much more about darkness and shade.

Camouflage by mimicry. This insect is hiding from a predator by mimicking a dry leaf.

Brilliant flowers in the understory.

Adaptations to shade take many different forms. But there are two kinds which are almost the opposite of each other. There are a) the adaptations designed to make something easy to find, and b) those intended to hide (camouflage) something.

a) Many of the plants in the understory develop brightly colored and beautiful flowers. Some of them are shown in the photographs on this page. This is partly a way of making sure they are seen by the birds and insects that pollinate them. Some plants also develop strong scents which attract bees and bats.

Bats are enormously important in jungles for the work they do in pollinating plants. The bats that feed directly on nectar or pollen do so at night. They are attracted by the scent of the flowers. As they suck up the nectar, they get pollen on their chests. This is then brushed off on the next flowers they visit.

Bats also have their own special adaptations so they can survive. For example, the West African fruit bat *Megaloglossus woermanni*, has a tongue more than 1in. (2.5cm.) long. This allows it to reach down inside flowers and take out the nectar. What makes this adaptation remarkable is that this species of bat is one of the smallest. It is only 3in. (7.5cm.) long. Its tongue is one third of the length of its whole body. (Try comparing the length of your tongue with your height.)

Similar adaptations are found in the beaks of hummingbirds and other nectar feeding birds. (See the drawing on page 17.) So the adaptations of the animals relate to the adaptations of the plants.

b) Adaptations designed to conceal can hide either predator or prey. For example, the common leopard has a spotted patterned coat. These markings merge with the dappling effects of shade and sunflecks. The leopard may be almost invisible from the ground as it lies stretched out on a branch of a tree. As its unsuspecting prey walks underneath it, the leopard drops down on top of it.

An example of the prey concealing itself is shown in the photograph on page 20. This is camouflage by mimicry. The insect is mimicking a dry leaf to great effect.

THE JUNGLE FLOOR AND SOILS

The jungle floor is the darkest and most humid part of the jungle. (See the diagram on page 11.) The air is very warm and almost always quite still. Explorers often describe the microclimate as "stifling" or "airless."

These conditions discourage most forms of plant life. Those that do live here are specially adapted. They are shade-loving herbs, tree seedlings and ferns. There is no grass. The photograph on this page shows what the floor is like. Even though some light reaches the ground here, because trees have fallen, it is still fairly easy to move around. It is interesting to compare this photograph with one of the jungle edge on page 12. Compared with most other forests of the world, the jungle floor is relatively bare.

The underlying soil is hidden by a thin layer of rapidly rotting leaves, twigs and dead flowers. They have fallen from the upper evergreen layers of the jungle. This litter layer rots very fast in the warm humid conditions. As a result, the layer is rarely more than 3in. (7.5cm.) thick, even though the evergreen plants overhead are always adding to it.

The work of decomposing or breaking down this litter layer is carried out by plants and animals that need little light. Fungi are the biggest group of plants. They live on the rotting remains of other plants. An example of a fungus can be seen in the photograph on this page.

Much of the work of decomposition is done by ants, termites and worms. There are many insects, including butterflies, in other parts of the jungle. But it is on the floor that the largest numbers of species of insects are found. It has been estimated that for every single species of backboned animal living on the floor, there are a hundred species of insect.

There are at least 240 species of just one kind of ant: the army ant. Different species of them are found in all the jungle areas. Unlike most other ants and termites, army ants do not have a fixed home, but move from

The floor of the Amazon Jungle. The buttresses of a large tree, the Ójè tree can be seen on the left. In front of the tree are some logs with fungus growing on them. On the right, the undergrowth is quite thick. This is where the collapse of a tree has let in more light. Elsewhere, there is little undergrowth, and the jungle floor is fairly open. Part of the litter layer can be seen in the foreground.

place to place. A single colony may contain twenty million ants all moving together. They move slowly at about 1ft. (30cm.) a minute so any active creature can avoid them. But anything injured or trapped or unable to move may be devored dead or alive. The insects and snakes of the jungle floor help to explain why almost every creature that can do so lives in the branches of trees. North American and European visitors to the jungle are easily persuaded to sleep in hammocks and to leave no edible possessions on the floor. As far as the ants are concerned, almost everything is edible, including books and clothing.

The animals of the jungle floor are usually shy and wary. They are prey not only for predators living on the floor with them, but also for the many others waiting to drop onto them from the canopy or the sky. (See the photograph on page 15.)

Some animals, like the Malayan tapir *Tapirus indictus*, are camouflaged. But the baby tapirs, which are rather like small pigs, have different camouflage from the adults. The Malayan tapir, like those in South America, are good swimmers and live close to water. This way, they can sometimes escape their attackers.

Other animals, like the South American peccary *Tayassu pecari*, seek safety in numbers. They graze in herds of up to one hun-dred. Peccaries are rather like pigs and root out bulbs and shoots. They have also been known to kill snakes and small animals caught by the herd.

Another way of surviving is shown by the royal antelope of West Africa. It is only about 12in. (30cm.) tall and is the world's smallest antelope. Just as a predator strikes, this small animal will leap sideways as much as 9ft. (2.7m.) in a single jump.

A few animals are protected by armor. The Giant Pangolin from West Africa is a good example, shown in the photograph on this page.

Below the jungle floor with its litter layer and many life forms is the soil. **Most jungle soils are surprisingly infertile.** Although they are very old and sometimes deep, the soils are **not** enriched by the rapid decomposition of the litter layer.

The correct explanation seems to be that in the struggle to survive plants take nutrients out of the soil as fast as they are produced. It is also true that many plants take nutrients directly from rainwater and from each other. Most of the nutrients in the jungle are found above ground in the vegetation.

Because the soils are so poor, **all** the plants struggle to survive. One result is a rich variety of plants. It seems that only in forests with fertile soils can one species of tree take over the forest. This is almost the opposite of what used to be taught in schools. It now seems likely that it is poor soils, **not** the rich ones, which have many different species of trees.

A Giant Pangolin *Manis gigantea*, Africa.
This animal lives on the jungle floor, where it feeds mainly on ants and termites. It can dig with its strong front claws and then extract the ants with its long tongue. It is about 5ft. (1.5m.) long and covered with an armor of scales.

Key words

decomposition – Rotting and breakdown of plant and animal remains.
litter layer – The layer of leaf and other plant remains on top of the soil.
nutrients – Chemicals essential for life; in this case, plant life. They occur in air and rain and are also produced by decomposition of plant and animal remains.

A fallen tree in the jungle. The fall of this tree has started the process of jungle turnover. All around the tree, new growth is filling in the clearing. A jelly fungus is already decomposing the old tree.

LETTING IN THE LIGHT

Below the jungle floor, with its litter layer and many life forms, lies the jungle soil. Although the soil may be rather infertile, it contains the most important part of the jungle. **It is called the seed bank.**

The seed bank is the small percentage of seeds that survived their journey to the soil. (See page 18.) They also survived the hunger of insects, and the disturbances by burrowing and rooting animals. Some of the seeds immediately grew into seedlings. Many others were buried.

This bank of seeds and seedlings, like money waiting to be spent, lies waiting for conditions to change. When these changes happen, the seeds burst into life.

The photograph on this page shows the first of these changes. A tree has fallen and left a small gap in the canopy. The amount of light reaching the ground has increased. Letting in the light is only the first step. Other changes now follow.

In the foreground of the photograph, a jelly fungus can be seen attacking and breaking down the fallen tree. As this process continues, two more changes will result from it.

First, the decomposition of the old tree will provide a huge amount of nutrients just when and where they are most needed. The new seedlings will be fed by the nutrients from the old tree. Second, as the old tree is decomposed, space will be cleared for the young seedlings to grow upward in the race toward the light.

Because the conditions at the jungle floor are warm and humid, these changes are very rapid. But in some cases, when a tree falls it pulls down its neighbors with it. The gap in the canopy may then be large enough not only for more light to reach the ground, but also more rain. This may speed up the process of change even more.

As the seeds burst into life, become seedlings and then small shrubs and trees, the clearing becomes filled with competing plants. This part of the jungle will now be impenetrable for several years. This process is beginning in the clearing in the photograph on this page. Travelers passing this way will either have to avoid this place or will have to cut their way through the new growth.

The first seedlings to emerge are often softwoods. They produce small trees reaching to the level of the understory trees. Later, they are overtaken and killed by the slower growing hardwood trees. The speed of these changes is so fast that in some examples studied, the fastest growing trees reached a height of 33ft. (10m.) in only ten years. They were then all replaced by the hardwood trees in the next ten years. In a total of twenty years, the gap in the jungle, or **pit** as it is known, has almost vanished. It has been filled in by new growth.

The final stage in the struggle toward the light is marked by one or two trees outstripping all the others. They become canopy or emergent trees. In the photograph on this page, there might be room for only one fully mature tree. The kind of tree that might win the struggle is shown in the photograph on page 17.

The unsuccessful trees will begin to die from lack of light under the re-closed canopy. The few survivors will be those adapted to be understory trees. The jungle floor will be in shade once more. There will be no dense undergrowth to obstruct travelers. (See the photograph on page 22.)

The process of tree collapse and replacement by new trees is known as turnover. **Turnover is the main way in which undisturbed jungle renews itself.** This process is now known to happen faster than was once believed. Scientists are now suggesting that turnover in the jungle may take only 130 to 150 years. This is very much faster than turnover in most of the other forests of the world.

If the light is let in by people clearing away a **large** area of jungle, the jungle almost never recovers. In the photograph on this page, which shows dry rice planting, the area shown is lost as jungle. Even if the land was abandoned, the forest that colonized it would not be true jungle. The secondary forest, as it is called, could not rebuild that delicately balanced environment. There may not be any secondary forest either, as soil erosion develops very quickly.

Malays planting dry hill rice, Sabah, Malaysia. An area of jungle has been cleared by felling and burning. The microclimate near the ground is now completely different.

Key words

colonize – To occupy, to take over, in this case by plants.
dry rice – Type of rice not grown in water. It is not grown in paddy fields.
hardwoods – Trees that give close-grained, hard timbers like mahogany. They are prized for their beauty and their resistance to rot.
seed bank – The collection of seeds and seedlings held in the soil.
softwood – Trees that give more open-grained timbers. Not all of them are soft. Balsa is the best known tropical softwood and is very soft.
turnover – The natural series of events by which dead trees are replaced by fully mature new trees.

SURVIVAL IN THE JUNGLE

The survival of any species depends on how well it is adapted to its environment. In the jungles, there are examples of every kind of adaptation. The fact that there are so many indicates that jungles have evolved over a very long period of time.

Some examples of adaptations are given in the diagram on this page.

If you look back at the first half of this book, and also at the diagram below, you will see that most species live in a state of crisis. **Crisis means danger and opportunity.** For example, most predators place themselves in danger when they go hunting. The predator can become the prey. A frog may be hunting insects only to be eaten by a snake. The two photographs on this page tell that story.

This state of crisis is a delicate balance. Animals are linked in food chains by eating each other, but they also live beside each other. This balance is sometimes self-correcting. For example, if too many snakes eat too many frogs, there will be a shortage of frogs. The snake population will either reduce in numbers because of lack of food or turn to other sources of food. Eventually, the frog population will increase again, until the snake and frog populations are back in balance. Life is a condition of interdependence. **Survival depends on adaptation and balanced interdependence.**

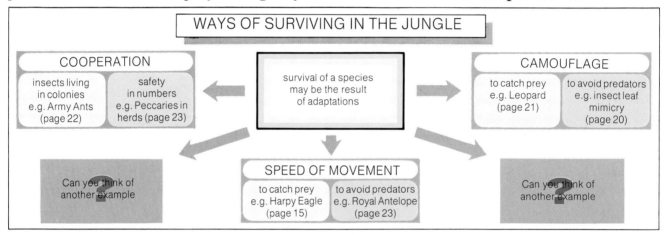

WAYS OF SURVIVING IN THE JUNGLE

survival of a species may be the result of adaptations

COOPERATION
insects living in colonies e.g. Army Ants (page 22)
safety in numbers e.g. Peccaries in herds (page 23)

Can you think of another example

SPEED OF MOVEMENT
to catch prey e.g. Harpy Eagle (page 15)
to avoid predators e.g. Royal Antelope (page 23)

CAMOUFLAGE
to catch prey e.g. Leopard (page 21)
to avoid predators e.g. insect leaf mimicry (page 20)

Can you think of another example

Hyla Frog meets Whip Snake.

Whip Snake eats Hyla Frog.

All species form a part of food chains. Even the top predators, such as leopards and eagles, contribute to food chains when they die. Their bodies fall to the jungle floor and are decomposed by insects and fungi. Then the decomposed remains supply nutrients to the soil. In this way, they complete a cycle by providing food for trees in which leopards and eagles can live.

Survival for many species is a combination of interdependence **and** competition **and** adaptation. One group of plants which show this very clearly is the stranglers. The strangler fig is the best-known species in this group. An example of a strangler using a tree for support is shown in the photograph on this page. The strangler develops through four stages:

1 A seed, perhaps dropped by a bird, becomes trapped in a cleft in a tree. It is adapted to live as an epiphyte.
2 The small plant puts out roots which hang down the side of the tree. At this stage the roots may look rather like a liana.
3 The roots enter the ground. The plant is now fed from the ground and grows much more quickly. It has adapted to being ground rooted instead of an epiphyte.

A mature rooted strangler on an old tree.

4 Eventually, it appears to strangle the support tree, which then dies. In fact, it probably kills it by being the more successful competitor for the nutrients in the soil. It may live for many years supported by the dead tree.

Finally, the dead tree collapses, and the strangler falls with it. It may continue to live for a little longer. But the main purpose of survival has been carried out. The species will continue because the strangler has given off several generations of seeds in its lifetime.

The delicate balance between life forms in the jungle is sensitive. If it is disturbed, the damage may spread to all aspects of life. The most serious disturbance is clearance of the jungle. As all the species are so fully adapted to jungle environments, they cannot survive anywhere else. Animals that can move away ahead of the bulldozers find themselves crowded together in the surviving areas of jungle. Here, overpopulation causes the deaths of many animals and even the extinction of some species.

Less spectacular disturbances can also cause much damage. The demand for parrots as cage birds in the U.S. is leading to a rapid reduction in the numbers in the Amazon jungles. It is interfering with several food chains. It may also have a severe long-term effect, as parrots play an important role in spreading seeds through the jungles. It may take a hundred years to recognize the effect of this disturbance.

1 Try to complete the diagram on page 26.
2 Check the meaning of the following words and phrases. Use this book and books from the reading list on page 43 to help.

environment	adaptation
survival	nutrient
competition	extinction
epiphyte	sensitive
overpopulation	food chain
interdependence	top predator

CHAPTER THREE

VARIETIES OF JUNGLES

FROM THE SEA TO THE MOUNTAINS

Travelers approaching jungle from the sea may find they have to wade through **mangrove swamps.** (See the photograph on this page.) These swamps are a variety of jungle in which the plants have adapted to living in a wet location. This location is a very special one. The mangroves are regularly flooded by salt water. The swamps may extend over a wide area along the coast, and inland to the full limit of the tide.

The trees that live in the mangrove swamps have adapted to the conditions by developing widely-spread stilt roots. They can be seen particularly clearly in the right hand side of the photograph below. This adaptation allows trees to get oxygen directly from the air. Very little oxygen is available in the waterlogged ground. The stilt roots may also help to stabilize the beach in which they grow. The travelers are aware of adaptation and interdependence even before they get out of their boat.

Inland sites which are waterlogged form marshy sites with trees quite different from those found in the mangrove swamps on the coast. Although some trees have adapted to these conditions, in many places only marsh grasses and aquatic weeds can survive. These evil-smelling marshlands are home to

Inside a mangrove swamp, Solomon Islands. This view shows the adaptation to stilt roots very clearly. The area in the foreground will be covered at the highest tides. Note how a tree has been felled to make a walkway.

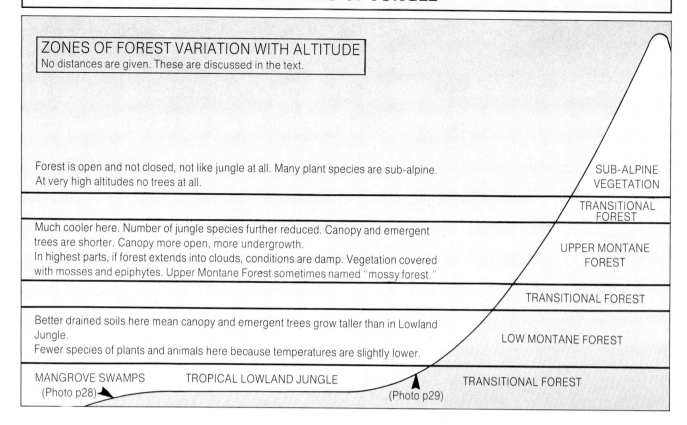

ZONES OF FOREST VARIATION WITH ALTITUDE
No distances are given. These are discussed in the text.

Forest is open and not closed, not like jungle at all. Many plant species are sub-alpine. At very high altitudes no trees at all.

SUB-ALPINE VEGETATION

TRANSITIONAL FOREST

Much cooler here. Number of jungle species further reduced. Canopy and emergent trees are shorter. Canopy more open, more undergrowth.
In highest parts, if forest extends into clouds, conditions are damp. Vegetation covered with mosses and epiphytes. Upper Montane Forest sometimes named "mossy forest."

UPPER MONTANE FOREST

TRANSITIONAL FOREST

Better drained soils here mean canopy and emergent trees grow taller than in Lowland Jungle.
Fewer species of plants and animals here because temperatures are slightly lower.

LOW MONTANE FOREST

MANGROVE SWAMPS (Photo p28)   TROPICAL LOWLAND JUNGLE   TRANSITIONAL FOREST
(Photo p29)

many reptiles and insects. In some parts of Amazonia and West Africa, great swarms of malaria-bearing mosquitoes breed in these places.

Jungles also show many variations in soils, angles of slope, the stage reached in turnover (see page 25) and altitude. Variations in altitude are shown in the diagram.

The boundaries between these different varieties of forest are difficult to relate to exact heights above sea level. There are two main reasons.

1 The forests change very gradually from one kind to another. There may be hundreds of miles of **transitional forest** between any two kinds of forest.
2 The boundaries vary with soils, steepness of slope, direction of rain-bearing winds and many other factors.

In much of Southeast Asia, the boundary between **lowland jungle** and **low montane forest** is at about 2440ft. (750m.) above sea level. The boundary between **low** and **upper montane forest** is at about 4880ft. (1500m.) But these figures do not hold true in other areas, such as traveling out of the Amazon lowlands into the Andes mountains.

Transitional forest, Peru. This area of jungle has all the features associated with jungle, but looks very different from the lowland jungle. Compare this photograph with others in this book. Make a list of ways in which the transitional forest is different.

THE JUNGLE EDGE

The edge of the jungle can be a place of transitional forest, or it can be a place of sudden change.

The diagram on page 31 is based on some locations in Africa. It shows how the jungle gradually changes to rainforest with a dry season (Seasonal Forest). This in turn changes into more open forest with grassland. Each of these environments may occupy many thousands of square miles.

The jungle edge at the waterside shows many variations. In some cases, the edge is quite sharp. This is shown in the photographs on this page and also on page 12.

The two cover photographs also show variations. The small photograph, taken in Sarawak, Southeast Asia, shows that jungle comes to the water's edge almost everywhere. There is just a small beach where the men are standing.

The large cover photograph is an aerial view in West Irian, Southeast Asia. It shows a strip of shorter vegetation following the river edge and separating it from the taller jungle. This different environment is partly the result of local people clearing the jungle from the bank. But in some places it is the result of riverside soils being waterlogged. Canopy trees cannot grow there. Compare this photograph with the one on page 12.

Where jungle and water meet, it is not only plant life that shows adaptations. Animal life is also changed. For example, some animals can live on land and in water. They are amphibians. Examples are crocodiles and, in South America, the world's biggest snake, the anaconda (*Eunectes murinus*). These animals are dangerous, but are hunted for their meat. (See the photograph on page 32.)

The jungle edge is often a place of opportunity. There are many different forms of life there. The local people can add fish and other catches to their diet. Or it may be a place where traders can meet. But the jungle edge shown in the photograph on page 31 is quite different. This is a place of danger, not opportunity. The delicately balanced environment of the jungle, with all its interdependences and adaptations, has been totally destroyed. Neither the jungle nor its inhabitants will ever recover from this kind of devastation.

How sad it is to compare that photograph with the one on this page.

Victoria Regia Lilies in Amazonia. The sharp boundary and difference between this environment and the jungle is clear. The lilies are rooted in the river bed, but the leaves and flowers float on the surface. The scent of the flowers attracts pollinating beetles. Local Indians collect the flower seeds and grind them into flour.

VARIETIES OF JUNGLE

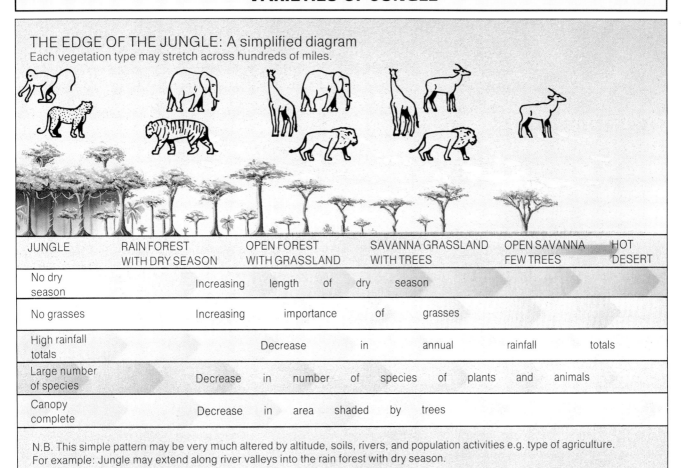

THE EDGE OF THE JUNGLE: A simplified diagram
Each vegetation type may stretch across hundreds of miles.

JUNGLE	RAIN FOREST WITH DRY SEASON	OPEN FOREST WITH GRASSLAND	SAVANNA GRASSLAND WITH TREES	OPEN SAVANNA FEW TREES	HOT DESERT
No dry season	Increasing	length	of	dry season	
No grasses	Increasing	importance	of	grasses	
High rainfall totals	Decrease	in	annual	rainfall	totals
Large number of species	Decrease	in number	of species	of plants	and animals
Canopy complete	Decrease	in area	shaded	by trees	

N.B. This simple pattern may be very much altered by altitude, soils, rivers, and population activities e.g. type of agriculture.
For example: Jungle may extend along river valleys into the rain forest with dry season.

The edge of the jungle. This is complete destruction and there will be no recovery from it. Apart from a few trees that may be dragged away for their timber, the jungle is destroyed on the spot by felling and fire. All forms of life are killed, except for the few that can retreat back into the shrinking area of jungle. Even the seed bank may be ripped out by diggers and tractors.

CHAPTER FOUR

PEOPLE AND JUNGLES

THE INHABITANTS

The inhabitants of the jungle lands live in a variety of different ways. However, all jungle peoples have learned one basic truth. **If they take too much from the jungle, their future is at risk.** Their lives are as fully adapted to the jungle environment as are the lives of the animals. This successful adaptation happens for two main reasons.

1 They understand the jungle. They are skilled hunters. They have great knowledge of jungle herbs, medicines and poisons. Much of their knowledge is useful to peoples in other lands.

2 They live in very small groups. Very few Amazon villages have as many as one hundred inhabitants. In Borneo, in Southeast Asia, Dyak longhouses are built for no more than fourteen or fifteen families.

In the jungle interior, life expectancy is short. Few people live beyond the age of forty. In parts of Amazonia and West Africa, fifty per cent of babies do not live to their second birthday. To the visitor, these facts seem terrible and need to be changed. But change affects how the people are adapted to the jungle.

Jungle peoples live a simple life in harmony with the jungle. The way they live divides them into two main groups.

1 **Hunter-gatherers**

The name describes the way they live. People living **only** in this way are found today mainly in the interior of the South American and African jungles. They rarely attempt to grow crops, but gather fruit, nuts and honey from the jungle. They may also harvest food plants that grow wild, such as wild rice.

A riverside scene in Amazonia, Brazil. These five men of the Suia tribe have caught an anaconda snake. Their families will eat well for the next few days. Fishing is also a vital source of food for jungle groups living close to the great rivers.

Nigerian village at the riverside. This picture shows how the village has grown in a jungle clearing at the riverside. This is a place where travel through the jungle by water is possible. There is also the chance to improve the diet by fishing. What do you notice about the building materials?

As hunters, they are top predators in the same way as leopards and eagles. They are at the top of the food chains. Because jungle animals are widely spread over large areas, the hunters need huge stretches of jungle to support them. For example, a family group of about twenty pygmies in Zaire, Africa, need about 200 square miles (500 sq. km.)

2 Farmers

For these people, slash-and-burn clearing of jungle is a vital part of life. (See the photograph on page 35.) The small clearings or gardens are planted with crops. But because jungle soils are so infertile, the crop yields decrease by about half every year. As a result, the farmers move on to new clearings. They are semi-nomadic. They may also add to their diet by hunting. This way of life is particularly destructive, reducing the size of the Amazon jungles. In some jungle lands, the larger rivers flood great stretches of lowland during the wettest season. For example, from May to July, the River Amazon floods a huge area known as the várzea. In several places, the river becomes more than 75 miles (120km.) wide. This flood environment is very important for the local people. As the water level falls, fish are plentiful. The flooded lands are left coated with mud on which good crops can be grown. This richer environment is reflected in the size of the villages. At the edge of the várzea, villages may have more than 2000 inhabitants. Villages in the jungle away from the várzea have up to 100 inhabitants.

The ways of life of jungle peoples are being very much changed by contacts with people from other areas. The photograph on this page shows a West African village in which the obvious effect of change is the building materials. Much more serious changes have affected and are affecting the people. These are discussed on the next page.

VISITORS AND INVADERS

Visitors to the jungles can be divided into two groups.
1 **People who come to *find out* something,** for example explorers and scientists.
2 **People who come to *take out* something,** for example loggers and miners.

This simple division is helpful in understanding what has happened and is happening to jungles. But it is not entirely true in all cases. An exploration by scientists may lead to the development of mining.

In the past the visitors to the jungle lands included European people seeking to carve out overseas empires. These invaders came first by sea as raiders and traders. The most tragic event was the West African slave trade in the 18th and 19th centuries. The British played a major part in this trade, and many slaves were shipped to the new North American colonies. Today, the descendants of those slaves are the black citizens of the U.S.

When the true story of slavery became known, public opinion helped to stop it. Today, as the true story of the destruction of the world's jungles becomes known, world public opinion can also help to stop this tragedy. Protests are becoming too strong to be ignored.

A first result of changed public opinion is that the two groups of jungle visitors are being given new and very clear labels.
1 The first group is becoming known as **conservationists.** What they are finding out is becoming a basis for saving the jungles.
2 The second group is still taking out from the jungles. The rest of the world is beginning to see them, not as helpful developers, but as **exploiters.**

Unfortunately, these two groups are both found in the governments of the jungle lands themselves. Some of these governments are destroying their jungles much faster than did the British, French, Spanish or Dutch when they were in control. Other governments, like the government of Cameroon, West Africa, are coming to recognize that what remains of their jungles needs to be conserved. (See page 38.)

It is easy to think of the struggle as:

CONSERVATION VS. EXPLOITATION

But the reasons for the continuing destruction of the jungles are beginning to change.

Jungle clearance by tractor and bulldozer in Nicaragua. The jungle is being completely cleared using modern machinery. This clearance plus the destruction of the seed bank will prevent the regrowth of jungle. This picture shows the nature of the jungle very well.

Greed is still the first explanation, but not the only one. Population growth is beginning to have an effect. As there are more and more people to feed, it is no longer possible to take a simple view of conservation. Simply to say "leave the jungles alone" makes no sense to the starving.

At every jungle edge, population pressure is increasing the demands for more farmland, more food. This is partly the result of **population increase.**

It is also the result of **population movement.** For example, in the Brazilian state of Rondonia, about 75,000 settlers are moved in every year by the government. Many of these settlers come from the more fertile lands of southeast Brazil. In many cases, they have been evicted to make way for new plantations and other large-scale farming developments. As the settlers arrive, they clear areas of jungle. Within two years, they can no longer feed themselves on the infertile and rapidly exhausted jungle soils. So they clear more jungle.

In some parts of Southeast Asia, the situation is even worse. For example, the Indonesian government has been evicting the peasants from their lands at the rate of about one million per year. Most of them have been moved out to the jungle and resettled on the lands that they can clear.

Today, an increasingly important reason for the jungles shrinking is the same as the reason for the hot deserts spreading. Population growth is getting out of control.

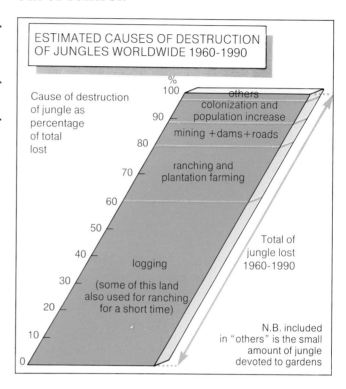

ESTIMATED CAUSES OF DESTRUCTION OF JUNGLES WORLDWIDE 1960-1990

Cause of destruction of jungle as percentage of total lost

%

others
colonization and population increase
mining + dams + roads
ranching and plantation farming
logging
(some of this land also used for ranching for a short time)

Total of jungle lost 1960-1990

N.B. included in "others" is the small amount of jungle devoted to gardens

Jungle clearance by slash-and-burn, Peru. A crop will be planted between the large tree trunks. After the people move on, the clearing may be reclaimed by the jungle. The seed bank is largely intact, and the many logs will provide nutrients as they decay. Closing this gap will take much longer than the usual turnover time. Compare this photograph with the one on page 34.

DESTRUCTION OF THE JUNGLES

The destruction of the jungles continues at a frightening speed. In the time taken to read a page of this book, the world loses about 250 acres (100 hectares) of jungle. In Amazonia alone, in the least wet season from July to October, an area of jungle the size of Switzerland is destroyed every year. As much again is destroyed every year in Central America plus Africa plus Southeast Asia.

The loss of jungles means the loss of all the balanced and adapted forms of life. The first half of this book showed how plants and animals depend upon each other. Destruction of trees leads to destruction of everything, including the people.

In Amazonia alone, 120 tribal groups of Indians have been wiped out in this century. Many of them have been murdered. The surviving Indians are not even classed as citizens in Brazil. They have no legal protection against having their homelands sold to the highest bidder.

In Sarawak, Southeast Asia, the Penan and Dyak peoples are organizing protests to try to stop the last of their jungle from being felled. The response of · the government, which sells the logging rights, has been to arrest protesters and imprison them without trial. They are described as agitators. Conservationists visiting the country are regarded as troublemakers.

Enormous sums of money are being made from logging. Other huge sums are earned through activities that replace the jungle, such as ranching, plantations, mining and contracts for road, rail and dam building. It is estimated that less than 25 percent of all this wealth remains in, or is returned to, the countries in which the jungles grew. Worse still, so little of this wealth ever reaches the inhabitants or displaced inhabitants of the jungles, it is difficult even to estimate the amount. In Great Britain, 10 percent of drugs available through its National Health Service have been developed from tropical plants. There is no record of the British Government ever making payment to any tribe which held this knowledge.

The destruction of the jungles benefit giant international corporations and the countries in which they are based. These countries are mainly the U.S., Japan and members of the E.E.C.

The destruction of the jungles of Sarawak is encouraged by the Japanese, who want the hardwoods for home use. The jungles of Central America and parts of Amazonia are

Clearing the Amazon jungle. This huge clearing is being prepared for cattle ranching. The land is quite unsuitable and will be abandoned in a few years. The secondary forest that will slowly fill the clearing will be quite unlike the original jungle. It will never support the rich variety of wildlife that once lived in the jungle. (Compare this photograph with those on pages 24, 34 and 35.)

being ripped out so beef cattle can be reared. Most of the beef for hamburgers goes to the U.S. In parts of Zaire, West German companies are destroying tracts of jungle for hardwoods for furniture and kitchen units. Most of these products could be manufactured as easily from some other material.

Even in Australia, the only developed country with its own jungle, the story is much the same. Conservationists have been blocking destructive road-building in some parts of Queensland. They have bravely chained themselves to trees or buried themselves up to their necks in the paths of bulldozers and tractors.

A few years ago, such people would have been called cranks. Now, public opinion is slowly changing. Gradually, the world is beginning to hear that:

1 Destruction of jungle is destruction of a non-renewable resource.
2 Jungle contains a store of life, of valuable plants and of potential medical cures.
3 Jungle destruction without reference to the inhabitants is always robbery and sometimes murder.
4 The effect of jungle loss is beginning to be felt worldwide, and not just locally.

Bougainville Copper Mine, Papua New Guinea. Mining developments are frequently justified by saying that the wealth produced will help the poorer people of the jungle. But they rarely see any of this wealth. Their experience of mining is all too often loss of their lands without compensation, plus the destruction of the jungle. Even in the case of the more carefully planned development shown in this photograph, damage is considerable.

PERCENTAGE OF JUNGLE SURVIVING IN 1985 THAT WILL BE LOST BY THE YEAR 2000

0%

INDONESIA

10

MALAYSIA
GHANA
GUINEA

20

COLOMBIA
BRAZIL
GUATAMALA
MEXICO

30

ECUADOR

40

NICARAGUA

50

HONDURAS
PHILIPPINES
THAILAND
ZAIRE

60

70

COSTA RICA

80

90

NIGERIA

IVORY COAST

100%

N.B. Indonesia has a further 60% of jungle set aside to resettle 17 million peasants made landless by developments elsewhere.

CONSERVATION OF THE JUNGLES

The jungles are in crisis. The crisis is leading to danger and opportunity.

The danger is clear. Half of the world's jungles are lost forever. Half of what remains could be destroyed by the year 2000. This loss not only impoverishes the jungle lands, but also the world.

The opportunity is that the whole world is being drawn into the struggle to save the jungles. The crisis for the jungles is a crisis for all of us. The good result of this new awareness is that **conservation is becoming an international effort.**

The two examples of conservation discussed on this page show the importance of cooperation between local people, their government, and international aid programs. **Korup National Park, Cameroon, West Africa.**

This is an area of coastal jungle of about 600 square miles (1000 sq. km.). In terms of animal life, it is the richest jungle in Africa. In October, 1986, it was declared a protected park.

There are four main reasons why this project is likely to succeed.

1 The government of Cameroon is strongly committed to a program of conservation.
2 The park is poor economically. There are no minerals, and the timber is almost impossible to get out across the rugged country.
3 The jungle people are fully involved in the project.
4 Overseas aid is available. The Overseas Development Administration of Great Britain is contributing funds. The World Wide Fund for Nature (W.W.F.) is matching this aid by voluntary donations.

The method being used in this project may provide a model for the rest of the world. In simple terms, the jungle is divided into two zones. There is an inner core of protected jungle. Outside it, and twice as big, is a buffer zone of jungle in which the people live.

In the buffer zone, the people are being encouraged to develop sustainable (long-

Buffer zone village in rain, Korup, Cameroon. This photograph was taken in a village in the buffer zone of Korup National Park. It is interesting to compare this photograph with those on pages 4 and 33.

term) methods of farming. The main method is agroforestry. This is crop growing with interplanted trees. The trees provide fruits, shelter, humus for the soil and protection against soil erosion. In addition, there will be some cattle farming and fish farming. These methods replace slash-and-burn farming and hunting.

In the core jungle, there is carefully controlled harvesting of fruits, nuts and medicinal plants. Further wealth may come to the people as controlled tourism is allowed to develop.

The project will succeed if:
a) The people now enjoy a better life in the buffer zone than they did in the past.
b) There is education for the people, especially in farming techniques such as crop rotation.
c) There is a sustained program of help and advice about birth control. If the buffer zone becomes overpopulated, the project will eventually collapse.

The possibilities offered by this project are so great that it may be extended across the frontier into Oban Park in Nigeria. (See the

Medicinal plant garden, Tambopata Reserve, Peru. The local people working with AMETRA are developing their skills in using traditional jungle remedies which had been neglected. In additional to collecting leaves, fruits and tree resin within the jungle, they are also creating small gardens like this so that more of the medicinal plants can be grown.

Extracting resin from the Ójè tree, Tambopata Reserve, Peru. This resin, like that of several other trees, plays an important part in the medicinal and medical knowledge of the local people. One use for this resin is in medicines to combat intestinal parasites, which are a main cause of infant mortality.

photograph on page 15.) The Nigerian government is beginning to realize that, at the present rate of logging, all its jungle will vanish by the year 2000.

Tambopata Wildlife Reserve, Peru, South America.

The Tambopata Reserve is 13,600 acres (5500 hectares) of jungle at the headwaters of the Amazon in southeast Peru. It was declared a reserve in 1977. Like Korup, it is an area of outstanding richness in its plant and animal life. It is also receiving overseas aid, especially through the work of the Tambopata Reserve Society (TRees) in the U.K. In most other respects, this Reserve is much less fortunately placed than Korup.

The biggest disadvantage is that the Reserve is very much smaller than Korup. As a result, there has been no chance to develop any kind of buffer zone. Logging and mineral rights have been granted right up to the edge of the Reserve. It is doubtful how many species of jungle life will survive in so small and threatened a jungle.

Another disadvantage is that the government of Peru is not very committed to con-servation. The Reserve is left unguarded. Poachers of both animals and trees frequently enter the Reserve.

The Tambopata Reserve does have one huge advantage. As a result of government mistakes, the Reserve partly overlaps the Indian reservation of Infierno. In this overlapping zone of 5000 acres (2000 hectares), a local branch of AMETRA (Applicacion de Medicina Tradicional) has been set up. AMETRA is concerned with the development of traditional medicines based on jungle plants. In this zone where both the people and the plants are protected, the work is flourishing. The health of the local population has improved dramatically. Many more medicinal plants have been brought into cultivation. The most important developments are the training courses to which people come from all over the jungle. The project is flourishing because local people are running it.

In the long term, both Tambopata and AMETRA need much greater support from the Peruvian government. In particular, a wide buffer zone must be created around the reserve if it is to survive.

CONCLUSIONS

JUNGLES AS A WORLD RESOURCE

JUNGLES ARE

evergreen tropical rainforests with no dry season;

old environments that have evolved over millions of years;

balanced systems in which all life is **adapted** and **interdependent;**

the **richest** environments in terms of **variety** of life forms;

large unexplored **storehouses** of plants with medicinal value;

fragile environments based on **infertile** soils;

environments with **many species,** but spread over large areas of poor quality lands;

capable of supporting only a **small number** of jungle people;

only able to renew themselves when the area cleared is **very small.**

Jungles are in crisis.
The danger is already clear.
The opportunity is becoming clear.

As the jungles are stripped off the face of the earth, the planet and its peoples are beginning to protest.

The disappearance of the jungles is a world problem. We have discovered that:
1 The jungles generate more than half their own rainfall by returning water vapor to the air. As this cycle is broken, the effects on climate are spreading.
2 Jungles produce oxygen, some of which enters the atmosphere. Jungles produce much more oxygen than open forests in other parts of the world. By clearing the jungles, we are beginning to choke ourselves.
3 Burning the jungles is not only reducing the oxygen supply. It is putting huge quantities of carbon dioxide into the atmosphere. This is adding to **the greenhouse effect.** This is the effect of pollution of the atmosphere raising temperature. The world is becoming warmer. It is now 1°F (0.5°C) warmer than in the mid-19th century. The "warmest year" record has been broken three times in the last ten years: in 1981, 1983 and 1987. The evidence is clear. If this trend continues until world temperatures have risen by only 9°F (5°C), the polar ice caps will begin to melt. Many of the world's cities and much of the best farmland will be drowned, leading to mass migrations of people worldwide. Climates will change everywhere.
There is no longer any sense in pretending the effects of jungle clearance are only local.

Tarantula spider, Tambopata, Peru.

Toucan, Amazon jungle, Brazil.

We are all entitled to be here in our jungle.

WHAT CAN BE DONE?

World opportunities

1 Encourage world opinion still more in favor of saving the jungles.
2 Rich countries must give up developing the wrong kinds of agriculture and forestry in jungle lands.

Out of greed, they have encouraged agriculture that will meet their own needs and not those of the local people. The worst example has been the influence of the U.S. on clearing jungle for cattle ranching. This land provides beef for hamburgers in the fast food industry. An American pet cat eats more beef than a Costa Rican peasant. The peasant cannot afford the beef because he has no job or land. They were taken from him by the international company that raises the cattle to provide the beef for the U.S.

Out of ignorance, rich countries and their agencies, like the World Bank, have encouraged "western style" growth in jungle lands. Foreigners need to support jungle peoples in **their own style of development**, one that does not destroy their way of life or the jungles.

3 The rich countries have to pay for the jungles NOT to be cut down.

A version of this idea is just being started. It is called "debt for nature." Instead of a poor government trying to pay its debts by logging and ranching, it leases a huge tract of jungle to the other country as a conservation area. This has recently happened in Bolivia and Costa Rica. Of course, this plan will only save the jungle if the new owners really care about conservation. A second problem is that if too much land passes to the U.S. and the E.E.C., they will have become exploiters again, but in a different way.

Jungle land opportunities

1 Developments like Korup and Tambopata must be encouraged. But they need to be much larger. It is estimated that a reserve must be at least 16,750 acres (25,000 hectares) for all species to survive.
2 Agroforestry in the buffer zones may enable the local people to enjoy a better quality of life while they cooperate in managing the jungle.

3 The jungle must be farmed and not mined for its timber. Logging can be restricted and controlled. Endangered species of trees can be protected. Carefully controlled selective felling might help to sustain the jungle instead of destroying it. Some of these possibilities are being tried out now in Malaysia.

4 Governments and local people need to cooperate more closely. The Brazilian government is currently meeting with Indian people in northeast Brazil to discuss their fears that dam projects will destroy their lands. At the same time, the World Bank has held back the loans it was going to make for the scheme. A government minister has publicly stated that he now acknowledges that 90 percent of jungle soils are unsuitable for agriculture. So far, all this is a matter of words rather than deeds. But attitudes are changing. Indians are beginning to be regarded as people with rights; jungle soils are being recognized as unsuitable for ranching.

Your opportunities

1 Join in with opinions and protests to save the jungles.

2 Put pressure on your government representatives. Countries that can send people into outer space can also find substitutes for hardwood furniture – if the people demand it.

3 Support stores that refuse to sell hardwoods.

4 Do not buy hardwoods. If you buy a hardwood stereo unit, YOUR hand is on the chain saw. If you do nothing, your hand might as well be on the chain saw. If you protest and act, you have taken your hand away from the chain saw.

Indians of the Amazonian Jungle, Brazil.

"The world has enough for every man's need, but not enough for every man's greed."

Mahatma Gandhi.

DO YOU WANT TO TAKE YOUR HAND
OFF THE CHAIN SAW?
There are several agencies working for the
conservation of jungles. Many rely heavily on
our donations and other forms of support.
Given below are the names and addresses of
three of these agencies. They are involved in
conservation work described in this book.

Conservation International
1015 Eighteenth Street, N.W.
Suite 1002
Washington, D.C. 20036

Friends of the Earth
530 Seventh Street, S.E.
Washington, D.C. 20003

World Wide Fund For Nature
1250 24th Street, N.W.
Washington, D.C. 20037

FURTHER READING

INTRODUCTORY BOOKS

Booth, Eugene *In the Jungle* Raintree Publications, 1985
Catchpole, Clive *Jungles* Dial Books for Young Readers, 1985
Cross, Wilbur *Brazil* Children's Press, 1984
Hintz, Martin *Living in the Tropics* Franklin Watts, 1987
Nations, James D. *Tropical Rainforests* Franklin Watts, 1988
Pimlott, John *South and Central America* Franklin Watts, 1988
Rowland-Entwistle, Theodore *Jungles and Rainforests* Silver, Burdett & Ginn 1987

MORE ADVANCED READING

Allen, Benedict *Who Goes Out in the Midday Sun? An Englishman's Trek Through the Amazon Jungle* Viking, 1986
Bates, Henry *The Naturalist on the Amazons* White Rose Press, 1987
Caufield, Catherine *In the Rainforest: Report from a Strange, Beautiful, Imperiled World* University of Chicago Press, 1986
Cousteau, Jacques-Yves *Jacques Cousteau's Amazon Journey* Abrams, 1984
Denslow, Julie (Editor) *People of the Tropical Rain Forest* University of California Press, 1988

Forsyth, Adrian *Tropical Nature: Life and Death in the Rain Forests of Central and South America* Scribner, 1987
Longman, Kenneth A. *Tropical Forest and Its Environment* John Wiley & Sons, 1987
Moran, Emilio F. *Developing the Amazon* Indiana University Press, 1981
Perry, Richard *Life in Forest and Jungle* Taplinger, 1975
Whitmore, T. C. *Tropical Rain Forests of the Far East* Oxford University Press, 1984

GLOSSARY

adaptation – an alteration that allows a plant or animal to survive in its environment.

Amazonia – all those lands drained by the River Amazon and its tributaries. (The name is often used to refer to all the South American jungles in central Brazil and the neighboring countries.)

canopy – the unbroken cover of treetops that makes a jungle a closed forest.

community – the plants and animals that make up the living part of an area.

conserve – save what is good and valued, hence conservation.

decomposition – rotting and breakdown of plant and animal remains.

deforestation – clearing forest from the land.

emergent – rising out of and above the canopy.

epiphyte – a plant that uses another as a prop. The epiphyte gets its energy directly from air and rain. It does not feed on the plant that supports it.

erosion – the breakdown and removal of rocks and soils.

evolve – to develop from an earlier form. (See adaptation)

humidity (humid) – the measure of how much water vapor is held in the air. The warmer the air, the more water vapor it can hold. We cannot see this water vapor. Inside jungles, the air is very warm. It holds a large amount of water vapor. We describe how this feels against our skin by using words like **humid,** sticky, close and muggy. If warm air cools down, it has to get rid of some of the water vapor. It does this by condensation. The vapor is turned into droplets, just as it is on your bathroom mirror. We can see these droplets as mist or fog or cloud. As warm air rises from the jungle, it cools and forms clouds. These clouds give rain. This rain returns the water to the jungle.

humus – plant and animal remains that have decomposed and contain nutrients ready for use as food for living plants.

jungle – a special kind of evergreen tropical rainforest. It is found in tropical areas with no dry season.

litter layer – the layer of leaf and other plant fragments on top of the soil.

microclimate – small local variation of the climate of the larger areas.

nutrients – any element or compound essential to life.

overpopulation – too many people or animals for the environment to support.

parasite – a plant or animal that grows and feeds on another. The other plant or animal, the one fed on, is known as the host. Hosts may be weakened or even killed by their parasites.

predator – a form of life that lives by hunting and eating another.

prey – a form of life hunted and eaten by another. In a good chain, an animal can be both prey and predator.

seasonal forest – forest developed in response to a climate with marked season, like a tropical rainy climate with a dry season.

seed bank – the seeds and seedlings stored in the soil.

slash-and-burn – a form of agriculture in which jungle is cut down and burned on the spot. Crops are planted between the fallen trees. Tree roots are not dug out, which helps protect the soils from erosion.

sub-alpine – plants associated with a mountain climate not as severe as that of the Rockies.

turnover – the collapse of old trees and their replacement by fully-grown new trees. The complete cycle takes about 130 to 150 years in jungle. In a temperate forest in North America or Europe, turnover may take as much as 500 years.

understory – the layers of the jungle between the canopy and the ground.

INDEX